Contents

Lists 49

Links   61

Images 71

Tables 79

Testing 123

Resources   129

CSS Quick Reference   131

Index   146

Introduction

This book was designed to help you find quick solutions to common CSS questions. The sections use a question-answer format, with a short description of the question, a visual example, and the CSS solution.

All of the solutions have been tested in Internet Explorer, Firefox, Opera, and Safari. Most of the CSS solutions are supported by the four major browsers, and notes are included when there is not a cross-browser solution.

Icons used in this book

The following icons are used throughout this book to help you find important and time-saving information.

Icon	Meaning	Description
⚠	Caution	Information about an unsupported CSS property.
◇	Note	Additional information about a topic.
TIP▷	Tip	A recommended best practice, shortcut, or workaround.

Updates

For the most up-to-date information about this book, see www.clickstart.net.

Overview

This section provides a focused, "to the point" overview of CSS.

What does "CSS" stand for?

"CSS" stands for "Cascading Style Sheets."

The word "cascading" is used because CSS formatting flows (or "cascades") from general rules to specific rules. For example, you can format the body tag to use black text. This rule will flow down to everything in your document, so you don't have to format each element (such headings, paragraphs, lists, and tables) individually to use black text. Each element will automatically inherit the black text setting from the body tag.

What is CSS?

Cascading style sheets can be used to format HTML, XHMTL, and XML documents. CSS is useful because it allows you to separate your content from its appearance. For example, paragraphs are contained within p (paragraph) tags, but CSS style rules specify how paragraphs are formatted. With CSS, a document's formatting can be easily adjusted for reading online or on paper, for viewing or listening (for hearing-impaired users), or for viewing on a PC or PDA. CSS even allows readers to adjust the text size if it's too small to read.

Who created CSS?

CSS was created by Bert Bos and Håkon Wium Lie. It became a W3C ("World Wide Web Consortium") recommendation in 1996.

Where can I view the full CSS standard?

The W3C prefers to use the term "recommendation" rather than "standard," but many people refer to their specifications as standards anyway. You can view and download the CSS recommendation at:

www.w3.org/Style/CSS

Where do I add my styles?

You can create inline, embedded, and external styles. Each of these options is described below, but here's a quick overview:

Type	Where it's located
Inline	Inside a tag
Embedded	In the \<head\> of a topic as a \<style\>...\</style\> block
External	In a separate css file

What are inline styles?

Inline styles are placed inside a tag:

```
<p style="font-family: Arial; color: red;">This text would be red.</p>
```

In short: inline styles are bad. They are hard to update, inefficient, and add unneeded code to your documents. For example, if you needed to change the paragraph above to blue text, you would have to find it in your document to change it to blue. That's not too hard for one paragraph, but it would be tedious to change 10 paragraphs. Imagine having to change 100 paragraphs in multiple documents. No thanks!

Another problem with inline styles is that you have to remember the formatting. For example, if you want to format paragraphs in multiple documents as 12pt red Arial, you have to remember those values. That can be hard to do with multiple types of content: headings, body text, notes, tables, bulleted lists, numbered lists, etc.

What are embedded styles?

Embedded styles are placed in the <head> section of a document:

```
<head>
<style>
p { font-family: Arial; }
</style>
</head>
```

This embedded style rule would format all paragraphs in the document to use the Arial font family.

The downside of embedded styles is that you cannot reuse them in multiple documents. You have to include the style information in each document, and you have to update each document if you change the styles. If you only have one document, you might as well use embedded styles. That way, all of your formatting and your content are in the same file. However, you probably have more than one document to format. That's when external styles become really useful.

What are external styles?

External styles are placed in a separate text document with a css extension. You can include multiple style rules in one external style sheet, and you can link multiple documents to the same external style sheet.

How do I link a document to a style sheet?

You can link a document to a style sheet using the **link** element:

```
<html>
 <head>
  <link rel="stylesheet" type="text/css" href="styles.css" />
 </head>
 <body>
  <p>Styles are cool!</p>
 </body>
</html>
```

How do I write a style rule?

A CSS rule begins with a selector identifying a target element. The selector is followed by a declaration block listing one or more properties of that element and a value to be applied to each property.

```
h1 { color: black; }
```

In this example, "h1" is the selector, "color: black" is a declaration, "color" is a property, and "black" is a value.

If you want to apply the same formatting to multiple selectors, you can separate the selectors with a comma. The following example applies the same formatting to h1s (heading 1) and h2s (heading 2):

```
h1, h2 { color: black; background: yellow; }
```

How can I easily format all of my content?

You can use the * (the "wildcard" or "universal") selector to format everything in a document:

```
* { color: red; }
```

Another approach is to use the body tag. A basic HTML document could be written as:

```
<html>
  <head>
    <link rel="stylesheet" type="text/css" href="styles.css" />
  </head>
  <body>
    <h1>Sample heading</h1>
    <p>Styles are cool!</p>
  </body>
</html>
```

An XHTML or HTML document contains two main sections: the head and the body. The * selector includes both sections, but the head section only contains "set up" information. There's no reason to format it because the user doesn't view it. So, the following style rules are basically the same:

```
* { color: red; }
body { color: red; }
```

How do I format a specific paragraph?

You can use a class or ID to format a specific block of content, such as a paragraph, list item, or table cell.

Classes - as many as you need

If you need to format multiple (but not all) paragraphs, you should use a class. For example, you might need to format three "note" paragraphs as red text. First, you would need to assign the class to each note:

```
<p class="note">This is a note.</p>
```

Then, you could write a style rule to format your notes:

```
p.note { color: red; }
```

This note class will first format a block of content as a paragraph and then change the text to red. If paragraphs are formatted as "Arial," your notes will be Arial and red:

```
p { font-family: Arial; }
p.note { color: red; }
```

If paragraphs are formatted as black text and your note class specifies red text, the note class will change your notes to red. Other paragraphs will still use black text.

IDs - one per document

You can only use an ID once in a document. You might use an ID to identify a copyright statement:

```
<p id="copyright">Copyright 2008</p>
```

You can then format the ID in your style sheet:

```
p#copyright { color: red; }
```

Generic classes and IDs

The class and ID examples above are both based on the p (paragraph) tag. You can create a class or ID for any element, such as heading 1s (h1), tables, or lists:

```
h1.pageTitle { color: red; }
```

However, classes or IDs that are created for a specific tag cannot be used for another tag. For example, the "p.note" class cannot be applied to a heading—It can only be applied to a paragraph.

You can create a generic class or ID that can be applied to any tag by not including a tag in your style rule:

```
.note { color: red; }
#copyright { color: red; }
```

This generic "note" class or generic "copyright" ID could be applied to any tag, such as h1, p, li (list item), or td (table data).

How do I format a specific word or character?

You can use a span to format a word or character. For example, to boldface the word "Start" in "ClickStart," you would first need to add a span:

```
<p>For details, see the Click<span>Start</span> website.</p>
```

You could format all spans to be bold:

```
span { font-weight: bold; }
```

Or, you could use a class to boldface only certain spans:

CSS rule
```
span.emphasized { font-weight: bold; }
```

```
<p>For details, see the Click<span class="emphasized">Start</span> website.</p>
```

How do I specify colors?

You can specify colors using rgb ("red-green-blue") values, hexadecimal values, or keywords.

All of these style rules would set the h1 tag to use red text:

```
h1 { color: red; }
h1 { color: rgb(100%, 0%, 0%); }
h1 { color: rgb(255, 0, 0); }
h1 { color: #ff0000; }
h1 { color: #f00; }
```

For a list of CSS color keywords, see:

www.w3.org/TR/CSS21/syndata.html#color-units

▶ *If a color's hexadecimal value uses pairs of numbers, like #aabbcc, you can use CSS shorthand to write the value as #abc.*

What happens if multiple rules apply to a block of content?

If multiple rules apply to a block of content, CSS uses "specificity" rules to determine which rule wins.

Inline styles override embedded styles, and embedded styles override external styles. For example, if a paragraph's inline styles specify green text, the text will be green no matter what color is specified in an embedded or external style rule.

IDs also override classes. For example:

```
<p class="sampleClass" id="sampleID">text text text</p>
```

First, the p tag's style rule is applied:

```
p {
  color: black;
  background-color: green;
}
```

Next, the class style rule is applied:

```
p.sampleClass {
  color: red;
  font-family: Arial;
}
```

Finally, the ID style rule is applied:

```
p#sampleID { color: yellow; }
```

The final formatting would be yellow (from the ID rule) Arial (from the class rule) text with a green background (from the p tag).

How do I override inline styles?

You can use the **!important** keyword to override inline styles. For example, you might have the following inline formatting in a document:

```
<p style="color: red; background-color: yellow;">text </p>
```

The following style rule will override the inline formatting in the example above:

```
p {
  color: black !important;
  background-color: white !important;
}
```

You must include the !important keyword for each property you want to override.

How should I order my rules in my style sheet?

You can arrange your style rules in any order.

Most CSS authors begin with rules for higher-level tags, such as * or body, and then rules for elements in the order they appear on the page: headings first, then paragraphs, tables, and lists. I often place my link styles near the top before the heading rules.

How do I add comments to my style sheet?

You can add comments to your style sheet between /* and */:

```
/* This is a one-line comment */

/*
  This is a
  multi-line
  comment
*/
```

Comments often include the author's name, last modified date, color definitions (e.g., "#aabbff is the light blue in our company logo"), and notes about browser issues.

Headings and Paragraphs

You can create up to six heading levels using the h1-h6 tags, and you can create paragraphs using the p tag.

How do I specify a font?

You can use the **font-family** property to specify a font.

```
p { font-family: Verdana; }
```

You can even specify multiple fonts. If the specified font is not installed, the browser will automatically try to use the next font in the list.

```
p { font-family: Verdana, Geneva, Arial, Helvetica, sans-serif; }
```

It's a good idea to end the list with a generic font. There are five generic fonts:

- serif
- sans-serif
- monospace
- cursive
- fantasy

Each generic font is assigned to a specific font family on the user's PC, so your text should appear in a font that is similar to the font you specified.

Which measurement unit should I use to size text?

You can use any of the following measurement units to size text.

Abbreviation	Unit	Relative or fixed?	Notes
%	Percentage	relative	
cm, mm	Centimeters Millimeters	fixed	Rarely used
em	Ems	relative	Sized based on size of uppercase "M"
ex	Exes	relative	Sized based on lowercase "x" Very rarely used
in	Inches	fixed	Rarely used
pc	Picas	fixed	Inconsistently sized by browsers Rarely used
pt	Points	fixed	Inconsistently sized by browsers
px	Pixels	relative	Often used to size margins and paddings, but not recommended for sizing text

You should use a relative unit for sizing online text. Users can resize relative-sized units, but fixed sized cannot be resized. Many users resize text to make it larger and easier to read.

The most commonly-used measurement units are ems and percentages. Percentages and ems very similar, but they use a different measurement scale. 100% is equal to 1em.

```
p { font-size: 100%; }
```

```
p { font-size: 1em; }
```

How do I allow users to change the text size?

If you use percentage or ems, your users can resize the text if needed. Fixed units, such as points, cannot be resized.

```
p { font-size: 100%; }
```

How do I set the color for text?

You can use the **color** property to set the color for an element.

```
h1 { color: #ff0000; }
p { color: #ff0000; }
span { color:#ff0000; }
```

If you want all of the text on the page to use the same color, you can specify the color for the body tag.

```
body { color: #ff0000; }
```

How do I add a background color to a heading or paragraph?

You can use the **background-color** property to add a background color.

Example

```
h1 { background-color: #0000ff; }
p { background-color: #0000ff; }
```

If you assign a background color to an element, the entire block of content will be highlighted rather than just the words. To highlight only the words, you need to use a span tag.

Example

CSS rule
```
span {
  background-color: #000000;
  color: #ffffff;
}
```

Usage
```
<p><span>Example</span></p>
```

How do I highlight text on the page?

You can use a span tag with a class to highlight text.

This·sentence·is·highlighted.

Note:·This·is·a·note.¶

CSS rule
```
.highlighted {
  background-color: #aabbff;
  color: #ffffff;
}
```

Usage
```
<p class="highlighted">This sentence is highlighted.</p>
<p><span class="highlighted">Note</span>: This is a note.</p>
```

How do I remove the space below a heading?

You can use the **margin-bottom** property to adjust the space below a block of content, such as a heading.

```
h1 { margin-bottom: 0; }
```

You can also use adjacent selectors to control the spacing between two elements, such as between a heading 1 (h1) and a paragraph (p).

```
h1+p { margin-top: 0; }
```

Internet Explorer does not support adjacent selectors.

How do I change the line height (leading) of my text?

You can use the **line-height** property to adjust the space between paragraphs.

text text text text

text text text text

text text text text

```
p { line-height: 200%; }
```

Or, you can set the line height for a specific paragraph.

CSS rule
```
.bigLineHeight { line-height: 200%; }
```

Usage
```
<p class="bigLineHeight">text text text</p>
```

How do I change word spacing?

You can use the **word-spacing** property to adjust the space between words.

text   text   text   text

CSS rule
```
p.wordSpacing { word-spacing: 10px; }
```

Usage
```
<p class="wordSpacing">text text text</p>
```

How do I change character spacing (kerning)?

You can use the **letter-spacing** property to specify the space between characters.

```
t e x t   t e x t   t e x t   t e x t
```

CSS rule
p.letterSpacing { letter-spacing: 10px; }

Usage
<p class"letterSpacing">text text text</p>

How do I left- or right-align text?

You can align text on the left or right using the **text-align** property.

```
h1 { text-align: right; }
p { text-align: left; }
```

How do I justify text?

You can justify text using the **text-align** property.

```
p { text-align: justify; }
```

How do I center text?

You can center text using the **text-align** property.

```
p { text-align: center; }
```

How do I indent text?

You can indent text by setting the **padding-left** property. Or, you can create a block quote by setting the **padding-left** and **padding-right** properties.

CSS rule
```
p.blockQuote {
  padding-left: 30px;
  padding-right: 30px;
}
```

Usage
```
<p class="blockQuote">text text text</p>
```

How do I create a hanging indent?

You can use the **padding-left** property to indent a block of content and the **text-indent** property to indent the first line. If you set the text-indent property to the negative value of the padding-left property, the first line of content will not be indented, but the additional lines will be indented using the padding-left property's value.

> text text text text text text text text text text
> text text text text text text text text text

CSS rule
```
p.hangingIndent {
  text-indent: -28px;
  padding-left: 28px;
}
```

Usage
```
<p class="hangingIndent">text...text</p>
```

How do I change text capitalization?

You can use the **text-transform** property to automatically change text to all uppercase, all lowercase, or title case (first letter capitalized).

```
.allUpperCase { text-transform: uppercase; }
.allLowerCase { text-transform: lowercase; }
.firstLetterUpperCase { text-transform: capitalize; }
```

How do I create a note style?

You can create a "note" class with a custom icon by setting the **background, padding-left,** and **line-height** properties.

 This is a note.

CSS rule
```
.note {
  background: url(pencil.gif) no-repeat left center;
  padding-left: 33px; /* min is width of image */
  line-height: 33px; /* min is height of image */
}
```

Usage
```
<p class="note">This is a note</p>
```

How do I remove page margins?

Browsers include a small amount of space around your content. Some browsers add this space with a default margin, and other browsers add the space using default padding. You can remove this extra space by setting the universal (*) selector's **margin** and **padding** property to "0."

```
* { margin: 0; padding: 0; }
```

How do I underline or overline text?

You can underline and overline content using the **text-decoration** property. The underline or overline can also be in a different color than the content.

If you want to apply a double or dotted underline or overline, you can use the **border-bottom** property.

Overline

CSS rule
.underline { text-decoration: underline; }
.overline { text-decoration: overline; }

Usage
<p class="underline">Underlined text</p>
<p class="overline">Overlined text</p>

How do I add a double or dotted underline?

The **text-decoration** property does not have a "double" or "dotted" value. Instead, you can use the **border-bottom** property to add double or dotted underlining.

Double underline

Dotted underline

CSS rule
.doubleUnderline { border-bottom: 3px double; }
.dottedUnderline { border-bottom: 1px dotted; }

Usage
<p><span class="doubleUnderline">text text</span></p>
<p><span class="dottedUnderline">text text</span></p>

How do I cross out or strikethrough text?

You can use the **text-decoration** property to add a line through text.

~~Strikethrough~~

CSS rule
.removed { text-decoration: line-through; }

Usage
<p class="removed">Sample line-through text</p>

How do I use a different color for underlines?

You can use a span to specify different colors for the underlining and the text.

CSS rule
.underlined {
text-decoration: underline;
color: red;
}
.standout { color: blue; }

Usage
<p class="underlined"><span class="standout">Sample red underlined text</span></p>

In this example, the underline is red and the text is blue.

How do I create a drop cap first letter?

You can use the **first-letter** pseudo element to format a drop-cap first letter in a block of content.

rop cap text text text text text text text text text text text text text text text text text text text text text text

```
h1:first-letter {
  font-family:Georgia;
  color:white;
  font-size:80px;
  line-height:60px;
  background:red;
  border:1px solid red;
  margin-right:4px;
  margin-top:4px;
  padding-top:2px;
  padding-right:4px;
  float:left;
}
```

You can also use a span to create a drop cap.

CSS rule
```
.dropCap {
  font-family:Georgia;
  color:white;
  font-size:80px;
  line-height:60px;
  background:red;
  border:1px solid red;
  margin-right:4px;
  margin-top:4px;
  padding-top:2px;
  padding-right:4px;
  float:left;
}
```

Usage
```
<p><span class="dropCap">D</span>rop cap</p>
```

How do I format the first letter?

You can use the **first-letter** pseudo element.

F irst letter

```
h1:first-letter {
  font-family: Georgia;
  font-size: 300%;
  color: brown;
}
```

Or, you can add a span tag around the first letter to change its formatting.

CSS rule
```
.bigLetter {
  font-family: Georgia;
  font-size:300%;
  font-weight:normal;
  color:brown;
}
```

Usage
```
<p><span class="bigLetter">F</span>irst letter</p>
```

How do I superscript or subscript text?

You can use the **vertical-align** property to superscript or subscript content.

CSS rules
```
.super {
  vertical-align: super;
  font-size: 60%;
}

.sub {
  vertical-align: sub;
  font-size: 60%;
}
```

```
<p>Blade Runner<span class="super">TM</span></p>

<p>C<span class="sub">8</span>H<span class="sub">10</span>N<span
class="sub">4</span>O<span class="sub">2</span></p>
```

How do I use Internet Explorer's filters?

Internet Explorer provides proprietary filters than can be used to format content.

 The filter property is only supported by Internet Explorer.

Alpha

The **alpha** filter can be used to make content transparent.

(white background)

(transparent background)

```
h1 {
filter:alpha(opacity=70, finishOpacity=0, style=1, startX=0, startY=0, finishX=200,
finishY=0);
}
```

You can use the **opacity** property to make content transparent in other browsers.

```
h1 { opacity:0.7; }
```

Here's a cross-browser example:

```
h1 {
filter:alpha(opacity=70, finishOpacity=0, style=1, startX=0, startY=0, finishX=200,
finishY=0);
opacity:0.7;
}
```

Property	Description
opacity	The starting amount of opacity (transparency) . 0 is fully transparent and 100 is not transparent.
finishOpacity	The ending amount of opacity. 0 is fully transparent and 100 is not transparent.
style	How the opacity is applied. 0 = uniform 1 = linear (beginning at the specified startX and startY position and ending at finish and finish) 2 = radial (beginning in the center and radiating out) 3 = rectangular (beginning at the corners and ending in the center)
startX	The starting x coordinate for the opacity gradient if the style is set to linear.
startY	The starting y coordinate for the opacity gradient if the style is set to linear.
finishX	The ending x coordinate for the opacity gradient if the style is set to linear .
finishY	The y coordinate for the opacity gradient if the style is set to linear.

Blur

The **blur** filter can be used to make an object appear out of focus.

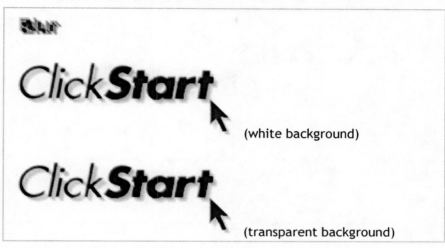

(white background)

(transparent background)

Property	Description
add	Specifies whether the unaltered image should be added to the blurred version. True=added, False=not added.
direction	The direction of the blur. The value moves the blur clockwise from 0-360.
strength	The amount of blur. The range is 0-10, and the default is 5.

```
h1 {
  filter:blur(add=false, direction=135, strength=6);
}
```

TIP *Unlike the dropshadow and glow filters, the blur filter is applied within non-transparent images, not around the image.*

Chroma

The **chroma** filter can be used to make a specified color transparent. This filter is often used with images.

(#00ff00 background)

h1 { filter:chroma(color=#00ff00); }

Property	Description
Color	The color that will become transparent. Hex value.

DropShadow

The **dropshadow** filter can be used to add a shadow behind an object. Unlike shadows, drop shadows can be applied in two directions. For example, a drop shadow can appear above and to the right of an object.

(white background)

(transparent background)

```
h1 {
filter:DropShadow(color=#aabbff, offX=5, offY=-3, positive=1);
}
```

Property	Description
color	The drop shadow's color as a hex value.
offX	The shadow's width in pixels. Positive values position the shadow on the right, and negative values position the shadow on the left.
offY	The shadow's width in pixels. Positive values position the shadow on the bottom, and negative values position the shadow on the top.
positive	Whether or not the drop shadow is enabled. True is enabled and false is disabled.

TIP *Unlike the blur filter, the dropshadow filter is applied around non-transparent images, not within the image.*

Glow

The **glow** filter can be used to add a radiant glow around an object.

(white background)

(transparent background)

```
h1 { filter:glow(color=#aabbff,strength=2); }
```

Property	Description
color	The color for the glow effect as a hex value.
strength	The intensity of the glow effect from 1 - 255.

TIP *Unlike the blur filter, the glow filter is applied around non-transparent images, not within the image.*

FlipH

The **fliph** filter can be used to mirror an object.

h1 { filter:flipH(); }

Property	Description
none	

FlipV

The **flipv** filter can be used to flip an object vertically.

h1 { filter:flipV(); }

Property	Description
none	

Gray

The **gray** filter can be used to change colors to shades of gray. Unlike the invert filter, the gray filter only changes colors. It has no effect on black or white areas.

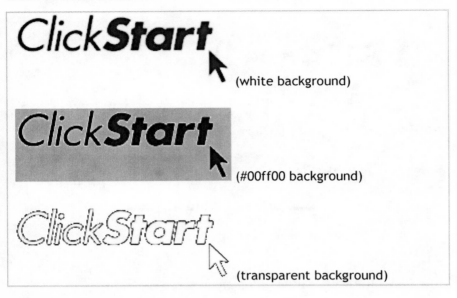

(white background)

(#00ff00 background)

(transparent background)

img.grayscaled { filter:gray(); }

Property	Description
none	

TIP *Unlike the invert filter, the gray filter does not apply to black and white areas.*

Invert

The **invert** filter can be used to reverse the saturation, hue, and brightness of an object's colors. It does not change transparent areas in an image.

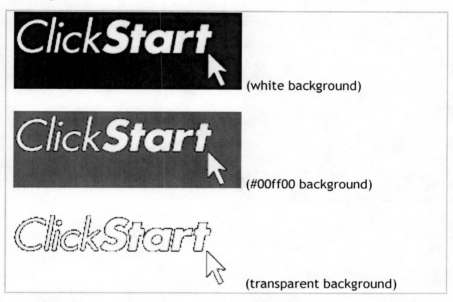

(white background)

(#00ff00 background)

(transparent background)

h1 { filter:invert(); }

Property	Description
none	

TIP *Unlike the gray filter, the invert filter applies to black and white areas.*

Mask

The **mask** filter can be used to invert an object and add a background color. In images, the colors are inverted and transparent areas are replaced with the specified color.

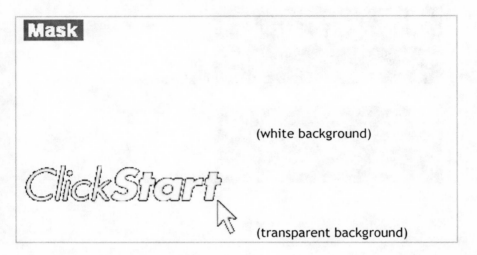

(white background)

(transparent background)

h1 { filter:mask(color=#aabbff); }

Property	Description
color	The background color as a hex value.

TIP *The xray filter has the opposite effect of the mask filter.*

Shadow

The **shadow** filter can be used to add a shadow to an object.

(white background)

(transparent background)

h1 { filter:shadow(color=#00cc66, direction=45); }

Property	Description
color	The shadow's color as a hex value.
direction	The direction of the shadow. The value moves the shadow clockwise from 0-360.

TIP ▷ *Unlike the blur filter, the shadow filter is applied around non-transparent images, not within the image.*

Wave

The **wave** filter can be used to vertically distort an object.

```
h1 {
filter:wave(add=0, freq=1, lightStrength=20, phase=100, strength=10);
}
```

Property	Description
add	Whether the filter should be applied. 1 adds the wave effect and 0 does not.
freq	The number of waves.
lightStrength	The intensity between the wave's peaks and troughs from 0-100.
phase	The angle of the wave from 0-360.
strength	The distance in pixels of the wave effect from 0-100.

Xray

The **xray** filter inverts black and white colors in an object. It does not change transparent areas in an image.

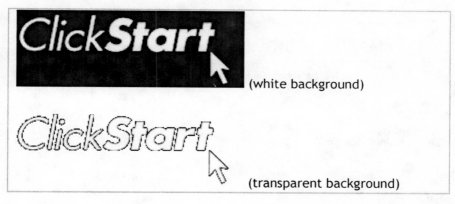

(white background)

(transparent background)

```
h1 { filter:xray(); }
```

Property	Description
none	

How do I create a shadowed box around content?

You can use Internet Explorer's **filter** property to create a box with a shadow.

This box has a dropshadow.

```
.shadowBox {
  width:200px;
  padding:10px;
  filter:shadow(color:gray);
}

.boxContent {
  width:200px;
  padding:10px;
  background-color:#ffffff;
  border: 1px solid black
}

<div class="shadowBox">
<p class="boxContent">This box is 200px wide.</p>
</div>
```

⚠ *The filter property is only supported by Internet Explorer.*

How do I insert content using CSS?

You can use the **content** property to insert content before or after an element.

To insert content at the top or bottom of the page:

```
body:before {
  content: "Confidential";
  font-weight: bold;
}

body:after {
  content: "\000A Copyright 2008";
}
```

To insert content before an element:

```
h1:before {
  content: ">> ";
  color: silver;
}
```

To add quotes before and after an element:

```
p.quotes:before { content: open-quote; }
p.quotes:after { content: close-quote; }
```

To add curly quotes:

```
p.boldcurlyQuotes { quotes: "\201C" "\201D"; }
p.boldcurlyQuotes:before { content: open-quote; }
p.boldcurlyQuotes:after { content: close-quote; }
```

The following table provides the Unicode values for special characters that can be inserted using the content property.

Symbol	Description	Unicode value
"	double quotation	0022
'	single quotation (apostrophe)	0027
"	double left curly quotation	201C
"	double right curly quotation	201D
<	single left angle quotation	003C
>	single right angle quotation	003E
«	double left angle quotation	00AB
»	double right angle quotation	00BB
`	grave accent	0060
´	acute accent	00B4

⚠ *The content property is not supported by Internet Explorer, and the quotes property is not supported by Safari.*

Lists

Lists are created using the ol ("ordered" or numbered list) and ul ("unordered" or bulleted list) tags. Each item in a list is tagged with the li ("list item) tag. You can format an entire list using the ol or ul tags, or you can format individual list items using the li tag.

How do I format nested lists?

You can use contextual selectors to format nested lists. The following table includes the contextual selectors for one level of nested lists.

Contextual Selector	Example

ol ol	• item 1
	  a. item A
	  b. item B
	• item 2

ol ul	1. item 1
	  • item A
	  • item B
	2. item 2

ul ul	• item 1
	  • item A
	  • item B
	• item 2

ul ol	• item 1
	  1. item A
	  2. item B
	• item 2

The following examples demonstrate changing the text color of nested lists.

```
ul ul { color: blue; }
ul ol { color: green; }
ol ol { color: red; }
ol ul { color: yellow; }
```

How do I add space above or below a list?

You can use the **margin-top** and **margin-bottom** properties to add space above or below a list.

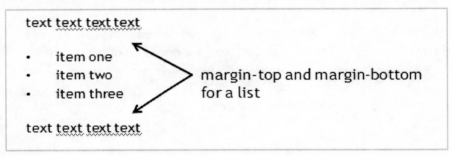

```
ul {
  margin-top: 20px;
  margin-bottom: 20px;
}
```

or

```
ol {
  margin-top: 20px;
  margin-bottom: 20px;
}
```

If you want to add space above and below both bulleted (ul) and numbered (ol) lists, you can combine them into one style definition.

```
ul, ol {
  margin-top: 20px;
  margin-bottom: 20px;
}
```

How do I add space above or below list items?

You can use the **margin-top** and **margin-bottom** properties to add space above and below list items. You should set both properties unless you want your list to be closer to the content above or below the list.

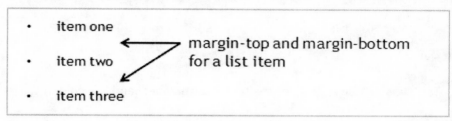

This example will add space above and below bulleted and numbered list items.

```
li {
  margin-top: 20px;
  margin-bottom: 20px;
}
```

If you only want to add space above and below bulleted list items, you can use a contextual selector.

```
ul li {
  margin-top: 20px;
  margin-bottom: 20px;
}
```

How do I format one item in a list differently from other list items?

You can apply a class to a list item to make it stand out in a list.

- item one
- *item two*
- item three

CSS rule
```
li.unique {
  font-style: italic;
  font-weight: bold;
}
```

Usage
```
<ul>
  <li>item one</li>
  <li class="unique">item two</li>
  <li>item three</li>
</ul>
```

The class will be applied to the bullet (or number) and the content.

How do I format the first item in a list differently from the others?

You can use the **first-child** pseudo element to apply formatting only to the first item in a list.

⚠️ *Internet Explorer does not support the first-child pseudo element.*

- ***item one***
- item two
- item three

```
li:first-child {
  font-style: italic;
  font-weight: bold;
}
```

For a cross-browser solution, you can assign a class to the first item in the list:

CSS rule
```
li.unique {
  font-style: italic;
  font-weight: bold;
}
```

```
<ul>
  <li class="unique">one</li>
  <li>two</li>
  <li>three</li>
</ul>
```

How do I change the bullet icon for a list?

You can create your own bullet icon and use the **list-style-image** property to apply it to your lists.

```
ul { list-style-image: url(arrow.gif); }
```

> item one
> item two
> item three

How do I change the bullet icon for one item in a bulleted list?

You can use a class to change the bullet icon for specific items in a bulleted list.

CSS rule
```
li.unique { list-style-image: url(arrow.gif); }
```

Usage
```
<ul>
  <li>item one</li>
  <li class="unique">item two</li>
  <li>item three</li>
</ul>
```

- item one
> item two
- item three

How do I left-align a bulleted list?

Browsers automatically indent bulleted lists. Unfortunately, some browsers indent bulleted lists using the **margin-left** property, while other browsers use the **padding-left** property. You can left align a bulleted list by setting both properties. Just don't set both properties to "0" or the bullet marker might not appear.

```
ul {
  padding-left: 1em;
  margin-left: 0px;
}
```

How do I left-align a numbered list?

Like bulleted lists, browsers also automatically indent numbered lists using either the **margin-left** or **padding-left** properties. You can left align a numbered list by setting both properties for the numbered list (ol) tag and for numbered list items (ol li).

```
ol {
  padding-left: 0px;
  margin-left: 2em;
}

ol li {
  margin-left:-.5em;
  padding-left: .5em;
}
```

TIP *If your list has ten or more items, the "1" in the number "10" will be too far to the left. You can assign a class to items greater than nine to adjust their margin-left property.*

How do I format list numbers?

You can use the **content** property to control list number formatting, including changing or removing the "." after the number and changing the size, color, or other properties.

1) item 1

2) item 2

3) item 3

```
ol {
  list-style-type:none;
  counter-reset: list 0;
}

li:before {
  content: counter(list) ") ";
  font-family: Arial;
  font-weight: bold;
  font-size: 14pt;
  counter-increment: list;
}
```

Note that the <ol> tag resets the counter to 0 because the li tag increments the counter before it is used.

This method does not work in Internet Explorer. A cross-browser method is to use span tags in your lists:

CSS rule
```
ol {
  font: italic;
  color: red;
}

ol span {
  font: normal;
  color: #000000;
}
```

Usage
```
<ol>
  <li><span>item one</span></li>
  <li><span>item two</span></li>
</ol>
```

Using this method, the ol tag's settings will be applied to the list number and the ol span's properties will be applied to the list content.

One advantage of the span method is that you can apply different formatting to selected numbers by applying different span classes.

CSS rule

```
ol {
  font: italic;
  color: red;
}

li.unique {
  font: italic;
  color: blue;
}

ol span{
  font: normal;
  color: #000000;
}
```

Usage

```
<ol>
<li class="unique"><span>This is line one</span></li>
<li><span>Here is line two</span></li>
<li><span>And last line</span></li>
</ol>
```

How do I start a list with a number other than 1?

The **start** property has been deprecated in CSS, but you can still use it to specify a starting number.

5. item
6. item
7. item

```
<ol start="5">
  <li>item</li>
  <li>item</li>
  <li>item</li>
</ol>
```

The recommended method is to use the **counter-reset** and **content** properties to specify a starting number. However, Internet Explorer does not support the counter properties or the :before pseudo element.

```
ol { counter-reset: item 5; }
li { display: block; }
li:before {
  content: counter(item) ". ";
  counter-increment: item;
}
```

How do I add a border to a list?

You can place a border around a list by setting the **border** property for the ul or ol tag.

```
ul {
  list-style-position: inside;
  padding: 4px;
  border: 1px solid #000000;
}
```

The **list-style-position** property is used to move the number or bullet inside the border.

How do I adjust the space between the list number or bullet and the list content?

You can set the distance between the list number or bullet using the li tag's **padding-left** property.

- item one
- item two
- item three

```
li { padding-left: 4px; }
```

How do I number headings?

You can use the **counter** properties and the :**before** pseudo element to format your headings with running numbers.

---

1. First Section

1.1 Chapter One

1.2 Chapter Two

2. Second Section

2.1 Chapter One

2.2 Chapter Two

CSS rules
```
h1 {
  counter-reset: chapter;
  counter-increment: section;
}
h1:before {
  content: counter(section) ". ";
}
h2 {
  counter-increment: chapter;
}
h2:before {
  content: counter(section) "." counter(chapter) " ";
}
```

Usage
```
<h1>First Section</h1>
  <h2>Chapter One</h2>
  <h2>Chapter Two</h2>
<h1>Second Section</h1>
  <h2>Chapter One</h2>
  <h2>Chapter Two</h2>
```

In this example, heading 1s are named "sections" and heading 2s are named "chapters." You can use other names if needed.

⚠ *Internet Explorer does not support the :before pseudo element for heading (h1 through h6) tags.*

⚠ *Firefox does not increment counters correctly if the counter-increment and counter-reset properties are set using the before or after pseudo elements. Instead, they should be set using the tag's base style (in this example, h1, and h2).*

How do I number headings and paragraphs?

You also can create "military-style" numbered headings and paragraphs using the **counter** properties and the **:before** pseudo element.

1. First Section

1.1 Chapter One

1.1.1 text text text text
1.1.2 new paragraph text text text text

1.2 Chapter Two

1.2.1 text text text text
1.2.2 new paragraph text text text text

2. Second Section

2.1 Chapter One

2.1.1 text text text text
2.1.2 new paragraph text text text text

2.2 Chapter Two

2.2.1 text text text text
2.2.2 new paragraph text text text text

CSS rules

```
h1 {
  counter-reset: chapter para;
  counter-increment: section;
}
h1:before {
  content: counter(section) ". ";
}

h2 {
  counter-increment: chapter;
  counter-reset: para;
}
h2:before {
  content: counter(section) "." counter(chapter) " ";
}

p {
  counter-increment: para;
}
p:before {
  content: counter(section) "." counter(chapter) "." counter(para) " ";
}
```

Usage

```
<h1>First Section</h1>
  <h2>Chapter One</h2>
    <p>text text text text</p>
    <p>new paragraph text text text text</p>
  <h2>Chapter Two</h2>
    <p>text text text text</p>
    <p>new paragraph text text text text</p>
<h1>Second Section</h1>
  <h2>Chapter One</h2>
    <p>text text text text</p>
    <p>new paragraph text text text text</p>
  <h2>Chapter Two</h2>
    <p>text text text text</p>
    <p>new paragraph text text text text</p>
```

⚠ *Internet Explorer does not support the :before pseudo element for heading (h1 through h6) tags.*

⚠ *Firefox does not increment counters correctly if the counter-increment and counter-reset properties are set using the :before or :after pseudo elements. Instead, they should be set using the tag's base style (in this example, h1, and h2).*

Links

t using the a ("anchor") tag. As
it links based on whether they have
s the mouse over the link.

ks?

matted as blue and underlined, and
rple and underlined. Links also have
, and hover. A link's state is "focus"
board, "active" when it is being
ser moves the cursor over it.

ecify how links should appear when
s. Since a link can have two states at
r hovers over an unvisited link), you
he following order:

HAte" (link, visited, hover, active) to

e the "focus" state. If you do want
to format the focus state, you should include it before active.

How do I change the color of links?

You can use the **link** and **visited** pseudo classes to change the color of unvisited or visited links.

```
a:link { color: #ffff00; }
a:visited { color: #0000ff; }
```

You can use the **hover** and **active** pseudo classes to change a link's color when the user is hovering over or clicking the link.

```
a:hover { color: #ff00ff; }
a:active { color: #00ff00; }
```

How do I remove link underlining?

You can use the **text-decoration** property to remove the default link underlining from all links or for one of the link pseudo classes.

To remove underlining for all links:

```
a { text-decoration: none; }
```

To remove underlining only for unvisited links:

```
a:link { text-decoration: none; }
```

How do I overline or underline links?

You can use the **text-decoration** property to add overlining to links.

My link

```
a { text-decoration: overline underline; }
```

How do I use a dotted underline for links?

You can add a dotted underline to links by using the **text-decoration** property to remove the default underlining and the **border-bottom** property to add the dotted underline.

My link

```
a {
  text-decoration: none;
  border-bottom: 1px dotted #000000;
}
```

How do I highlight a link when the user hovers their mouse over it?

You can set the **background-color** property for the hover and active pseudo classes. The hover pseudo class sets the highlight color when the mouse is hovering over the link, and the active pseudo class sets the highlight color when the user clicks the link.

```
a:hover, a:active {
  color: #FF0000;
  background-color: #FFFF00;
}
```

How do I mark visited links?

You can automatically include an icon for visited links to show the user which links they've clicked.

 My link

```
a:visited {
  background: url(checked.png) right center no-repeat;
  padding-right: 20px; }
```

You can even use the hover pseudo class to change the link icon when the user hovers over the visited link.

✓ My link

```
a:visited:hover {
  background-image: url(checkHover.png) right center no-repeat;
  padding-right: 20px;
}
```

In these examples, the image is 12px. The padding-right property has been set to 20px to offset the icon from the link text.

How do I show link paths when the user prints the page?

You can include an **@media print** rule in your style sheet to specify different property values for print. See the "Print" chapter on page 99 for more tips about using @media print.

Visit <u>our website</u> (http://www.clickstart.net) for more tips.

```
@media print {
  a:link:after, a:visited:after {
    content: " (" attr(href) ") ";
  }
}
```

⚠ *Internet Explorer does not support the content property.*

How do I use special formatting for external or email links?

You can use attribute selectors with the a ("anchor" or link) tag to format external or email links.

Send us an email at info@clickstart.net 📧 for more information.

To format external links:

```
a[href^="http:"] {
  background: url(weblink.png) right center no-repeat;
  padding-right: 20px;
}
```

To format email links:

```
a[href^="mailto:"] {
  background: url(email.png) right center no-repeat;
  padding-right: 20px;
}
```

Attribute selectors are not supported by Internet Explorer. For a cross-browser solution, you can format your external and email links using classes.

```
a.webLink {
  background: url(web.png) right center no-repeat;
  padding-right: 20px;
}
```

```
a.emailLink {
  background: url(email.png) right center no-repeat;
  padding-right: 20px;
}
```

In these examples, the image is 12px. The padding-right property has been set to 20px to offset the icon from the link text.

How can I include an icon for ZIP, PDF, DOC, or PPT links?

You can use attribute selectors to automatically include an icon for selected file types.

For more information, open the <u>User's Guide</u> ⊠ Word document.

```
a[href$=".pdf"] {
  background: url(pdf.png) right center no-repeat
  padding-right: 20px;
}

a[href$=".doc"] {
  background: url(word.png) right center no-repeat;
  padding-right: 20px;
}
```

Attribute selectors are not supported by Internet Explorer. For a cross-browser solution, you can format your links with classes.

CSS rule
```
a.wordDoc {
  background: url(word.png) right center no-repeat;
  padding-right: 20px;
}
```

```
<a class="wordDoc" href="myWordDoc.doc">link text</a>
```

In these examples, the image is 12px. The padding-right property has been set to 20px to offset the icon from the link text.

TIP *The following website provides some icons you can use for your links: www.stylegala.com/features/bulletmadness*

How do I remove the dotted lines around an active link?

Most browsers add a dotted line border around an active link ("active" means when you are clicking the link). You can use the **focus** pseudo class and the **outline** property to remove the dotted line border.

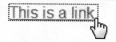

```
a:focus { outline: none; }
```

 Internet Explorer does not support the outline property.

How do I create a link that looks like a button?

You can use the **border** and **background** properties to make a link look like a button.

`My link`

```
a {
  display: block;
  border: 1px solid;
  border-color: #aaa #000 #000 #aaa;
  width: 8em;
  background: #fc0;
}

a:hover {
  position: relative;
  top: 1px;
  left: 1px;
  border-color: #000 #aaa #aaa #000;
}
```

TIP▶ *This example uses CSS shorthand to assign colors. For example, #abc is shorthand for #aabbcc.*

How do I display the help cursor?

You can specify the help cursor for all links, for specific links, or for any other element.

To show the help cursor for all links:

```
a { cursor: help; }
```

To show the help cursor for specific links using a class:

```
a.cursorHelp { cursor: help; }
```

To show the help cursor for other elements:

```
h1 { cursor: help; }
```

How do I change the cursor?

You can use the **cursor** property to display the following icons:

Value	Example Icon
auto	Automatically changes based on what the user is doing.
default	
all-scroll	
col-resize	
crosshair	
help	
move	
e-resize	
n-resize	

Value	Example Icon
ne-resize	↗
nw-resize	↖
s-resize	↕
se-resize	↘
sw-resize	↙
w-resize	↔
no-drop	🖐⊘
not-allowed	⊘
pointer	👆
progress	⌛
row-resize	⬍
text	I
vertical-text	⊢⊣
wait	⌛

How do I use my own cursor icon?

You can also create and use your own cursor icon. Your cursor image must be a .cur or .ani file.

```
a { cursor: url(bigArrow.cur); }
```

> TIP▶ *The following website provides some icons you can use as a cursor: www.javascriptkit.com/dhtmltutors/csscursors.shtml*

Images

You can add images to your documents using the img tag, or you can add a background image to the entire document.

How do I set a background image for my page?

You can use body tag's **background-image** property to set a background image for the entire page.

> # Background
>
> text text text text text text text text text text text text text text text text text text text text text text text text text text text text text text text text text text text text text text text text text text text text text text text text text text text text text text text text text text text text

```
body { background-image: url('draft.gif'); }
```

How do I position my background image?

You can use the **background-position** property to specify where your background image will appear.

Background

text text text text text text text text text text text text text text text text text text text text text text text text text text text text text text text text text text text text text text text text text text text text text text text text text text text text text text text text text text text text text text text text text text text text

```
body {
  background-image: url('draft.gif');
  background-position: bottom right;
  background-repeat: no-repeat;
}
```

You can use the following keyword combinations with the background-position property:

Keywords		
top left	center left	bottom left
top center	center center	bottom center
top right	center right	bottom right

These keywords can be written in either order. For example, "top left" and "left top" will both work correctly. If you only specify one value, the other value will default to center.

You can also use percentages to set the position.

```
background-position: 30% 80%;
```

0% 0% would position the image in the top left, and 100% 100% would position it in the bottom right. Setting the background-position to 50% 50% would center the image, as would center center.

The following list shows how keyword settings match percentage settings:

Keywords	Percentages
left top	0% 0%
center top	50% 0%
right top	100% 0%
left center	0% 50%
center center	50% 50%
right center	100% 50%
left bottom	0% 100%
center bottom	50% 100%
right bottom	100% 100%

If you use keywords or percentages, your background image's position will adjust to the size of the window. You can also use pixels to set a non-adjusting position:

```
background-position: 20px 20px;
```

How do I fix my background image so it doesn't scroll?

You can use the **background-attachment** property to fix an image in place and prevent it from scrolling with rest of the page's content.

```
body {
    background-attachment: fixed;
    background-image: url('draft.gif');
    background-position: 50% 50%;
    background-repeat: no-repeat;
}
```

⚠ *The background-attachment property was not fully supported in past versions of Internet Explorer. It is fully supported by Internet Explorer 7 and later.*

Value	Description
repeat	The background repeats horizontally and vertically. This is the default setting.
repeat-x	The background repeats horizontally but not vertically.
repeat-y	The background repeats vertically bit not horizontally.
no-repeat	The background does not repeat horizontally or vertically.

How do I add more than one background image to my document?

You can use more than one background image by applying one image to the html tag and another to the body tag.

Background

text text text text text text text text text text text text text text text text text text text text text text text text text text text text text text text text text text text text text text text text text text text text text text text text text text text text text text text text text text text

© 2019 TYRELL CORP

```
html {
  background-image: url('logo.gif');
  background-position: bottom right;
  background-repeat: no-repeat;
}

body {
  background-attachment: fixed;
  background-image: url('draft.gif');
  background-position: 50% 50%;
  background-repeat: no-repeat;
}
```

How do I wrap text around an image?

You can use the **float** property to wrap text around an image.

 caution

CSS rule
```
.caution {
  float: left;
  margin-right: 10px;
}
```

Usage
```
<p><img class="caution" src="caution.jpg" />
caution caution caution</p>
```

The **margin-left** property can be used to add space between the image and the text.

How do I place text on top of an image?

You can assign negative values to the **position**, **top**, and **left** properties to position text on top of an image. If the text is below the image, setting its top property to a negative value will move the text on top of the image.

```
.overlap {
  position: relative;
  top: -200px;
  left: 180px;
  color: #ffffff;
}
```

Usage

```
<img src="sample.jpg" />
<p class="overlap">floating text</p>
```

How do I add a border to an image?

Borders are most often used with tables, but you can also add borders to images using the **border** properties.

```
img {
  border-width: 3px;
  border-style: solid;
  border-color: #000000;
}
```

You can also use CSS shorthand to specify borders:

```
img { border: 1px solid #000000; }
```

The examples above will add a border to all images. You can create a class if you want to apply borders only to specified images.

```
.imgBorder { border: 1px solid #000000; }
```

```
<img class="imgBorder" src="sampleImage.jpg" />
```

Or, you can apply a border to all images inside a div tag:

CSS rule

```
#menuBar img { border: 1px solid #000000; }
```

Usage

```
<div id="menuBar"><img src="sampleImage.jpg" /></div>
```

How do I remove link borders from images?

You can set an image's **border** property to "0" to remove the border that appears around image links by default.

```
img { border: 0; }
```

How do I zoom images when the user hovers over them?

If you wrap a link around an image, you can use the link's hover pseudo class to change the image's width and height.

First, wrap a link around the image:

```
<a href="javascript:void(0);">
  <img src="clickstart.jpg" />
</a>
```

Then, specify the image's width and height when the user hovers over the image's link.

```
a:hover img { width: 800px; height: 400px; }
```

In this example, the image will expand to 800x400 when the user hovers over the image, and it will return to its original size when the user moves the mouse away from the image.

How do I add a drop shadow to an image?

You can use Internet Explorer's **filter** property to add a drop shadow to an image. The filter property was created by Microsoft and is not a part of the CSS recommendation. It is only supported by Internet Explorer.

For more information about Internet Explorer filters, see "How do I use Internet Explorer's filters?" on page 33.

```
img {
  filter: progid:DXImageTransform.Microsoft.dropShadow (offX='3', offY='5',
  color='#c0c0c0', positive='true');
}
```

How do I make an image transparent?

You can use Internet Explorer's **alpha** filter to make an image transparent. For other browsers, you can use the **opacity** property.

```
img {
  filter:alpha(opacity=50);
  opacity:.50;
}
```

How do I apply Internet Explorer's filters to images?

See "How do I use Internet Explorer's filters?" on page 33.

Tables

You can create tables using the table tag. Each row in a table is placed inside a tr ("table row") tag, each table header is inside a th tag, and each non-header ("data") row is placed inside tr a tag:

```
<table>
  <tr>
    <th>table header</th>
    <th>table header</th>
  </tr>
  <tr>
    <td>text text text</td>
    <td>text text text</td>
  </tr>
</table>
```

How do I center a table?

You can center a table by setting the **margin-left** and **margin-right** properties to "auto."

```
table {
  margin-left: auto;
  margin-right: auto;
}
```

How do I left- or right-align a table?

You can left- or right-align a table by setting the **margin-left** or **margin-right** property to "0."

```
table {
  margin-left: 0;
  margin-right: auto;
}
```

How do I center content inside a table?

You can center a table's content using the **text-align** property.

Winner	Score	Loser
West Germany	1-0	Poland
Netherlands	2-0	Brazil
Poland	1-0	Brazil
West Germany	2-1	Netherlands

th, td { text-align: center; }

This example centers the table header (using the th tag) and the table data (using the td tag).

How do I center content vertically inside a table?

You can use the **valign** property to vertically align content in a table.

Winner	Score	Loser
West Germany	1-0	Poland
Netherlands	2-0	Brazil
Poland	1-0	Brazil
West Germany	2-1	Netherlands

th, td { valign: middle; }

How do I left- or right-align content inside a table?

You can use the **text-align** property to left- or right-align a table's contents.

Winner	Score	Loser
West Germany	1-0	Poland
Netherlands	2-0	Brazil
Poland	1-0	Brazil
West Germany	2-1	Netherlands

th, td { text-align: right; }

How do I add table borders?

You can add borders using the **border-style** property.

Border value	Example
solid	
dashed	
dotted	
double	
groove	
inset	
outset	
ridge	

table { border: 8px groove blue; }

You can specify different colors, styles, and widths for the top, right, bottom, and left borders.

```
table {
  border-right: 1px solid #ff0000;
  border-top: 4px solid #ff0000;
}
```

How do I remove the space between table cells' borders?

Table borders can have a 3D effect if you use cell and table borders. You can remove the thin space between your table borders and cell borders by setting the **border-collapse** property.

Winner	Score	Loser
West Germany	1-0	Poland
Netherlands	2-0	Brazil
Poland	1-0	Brazil
West Germany	2-1	Netherlands

```
table { border-collapse: collapse; }
```

How do I use different colors for the outside and inside borders?

If you use the border-collapse property to combine your table borders and cell borders, the wider border will be used for the outer border. If the table and cell borders are set to the same width, the cell borders will be used for the outer (table) borders.

If your table and cell borders are the same width, you can use the **border-style** property to specify different colors for the outer table borders and the inner cell borders.

```
table {
  border-collapse: collapse;
  border-color: #00ff00;
  border-style: solid;
  border-width: 1px;
}

th, td {
  border-color: #ff0000;
  border-style: inset;
  border-width: 1px;
}
```

In this example, the table tag's border-style property is set to "solid" and the th and td tags are set to "inset." The border-style properties values are ranked as follows:

double, solid, dashed, dotted, ridge, outset, groove, and inset (the lowest)

Setting the table tag's border style to "solid" gives it precedence over the th and td tag's "inset" value.

How do I keep content inside my table from touching the borders?

You can use the **padding** property to prevent the table's content from touching the table's border.

```
th, td { padding: 2px; }
```

In this example, the th tag is used to set the table header's padding, and the td tag is used to set the table data and table footer's padding.

How do I format table rows with alternating background colors?

You have three options for formatting tables with alternating row background colors:

- classes
- tr:nth-child pseudo element
- JavaScript

Winner	Score	Loser
West Germany	1-0	Poland
Netherlands	2-0	Brazil
Poland	1-0	Brazil
West Germany	2-1	Netherlands

Using classes

One option is to assign a class to every other row in the table. The downside is that you have to apply the class to each row yourself, and you have to update it if you add or remove rows.

CSS rule

```
tr.altRow {
  background-color: #0000ff;
  color: #ffffff;
}
```

Usage

```
<tr>
...
</tr>
<tr class="altRow">
  <td>Netherlands</td>
  <td>2-0</td>
  <td>Brazil</td>
</tr>
```

Using the tr:nth-child pseudo element

Another option is to use the **tr:nth-child** pseudo element. However, the tr:nth-child pseudo element is not supported by Internet Explorer, Firefox, or Opera. It is supported by Safari.

CSS rule
```
tr:nth-child(even) {
  background-color: #0000ff;
  color: #ffffff;
}
```

Usage
```
<tr>
  <td>West Germany</td>
  <td>1-0</td>
  <td>Poland</td>
</tr>
<tr>
  <td>Netherlands</td>
  <td>2-0</td>
  <td>Brazil</td>
</tr>
```

Using JavaScript

A third option is to use JavaScript to find alternating rows and apply the class. See the JavaScript Tips page at www.clickstart.net for a script you can use.

How do I highlight a cell in a table?

You can highlight a cell in a table by applying a class to its td (table data) tag.

Winner	Score	Loser
West Germany	1-0	Poland
Netherlands	2-0	Brazil
West Germany	2-1	Netherlands

```
td.highlighted {
background-color: #ffff00;
}
```

Usage

```
<tr>
 <td>West Germany</td>
 <td class="highlighted">2-1</td>
 <td>Netherlands</td>
</tr>
```

How do I highlight one row in a table?

You can highlight a row in a table by applying a class to its tr (table row) tag.

Winner	Score	Loser
West Germany	1-0	Poland
Netherlands	2-0	Brazil
Poland	1-0	Brazil
West Germany	2-1	Netherlands

CSS rule

tr.highlighted { background-color: #ffff00; }

Usage

```
<tr class="highlighted">
 <td>West Germany</td>
 <td>2-1</td>
 <td>Netherlands</td>
</tr>
```

How do I change a row's background color on hover?

You can use the **hover** pseudo class to change a row's background color when the user's mouse is over the row. Pseudo classes are often used with links, but they can also be used with other tags.

```
tr:hover { background-color: #ffff00; }
```

Since table headers are also considered table rows, they will also highlight on hover. If you don't want your header row(s) to highlight, you can specify a background color for the th tag.

```
th { background-color: #ffffff; }
tr:hover { background-color: #ffff00; }
```

⚠ *Internet Explorer only supports the hover pseudo class with links—it is ignored for other tags.*

How do I change a cell's background color on hover?

You can also use the **hover** pseudo class to change a cell's background color.

```
td:hover { background-color: #ffff00; }
```

Since table headers use the th (table header) tag rather than the td tag, table headers will not change using td:hover. If you want to highlight a table header on hover, use th:hover instead:

```
th:hover { background-color: #ffff00; }
```

⚠ *Internet Explorer only supports the hover pseudo class with links—it is ignored for other tags.*

How do I set a background color for a table?

You can use the **background** property to set a table's background color.

```
table { background: #ff0000; }
```

How do I use an image as a table's background?

You can also use the **background** property to use an image for a table's background.

Winner	Score	Loser
West Germany	1-0	Poland
Netherlands	2-0	Brazil
Poland	1-0	Brazil
West Germany	2-1	Netherlands

```
table { background: url(background.jpg); }
```

How do I use a gradient for a table's background color?

You can use Internet Explorer's **filter** property to create background gradients. However, this non-standard CSS property is only supported by Internet Explorer.

Winner	Score	Loser
West Germany	1-0	Poland
Netherlands	2-0	Brazil
Poland	1-0	Brazil
West Germany	2-1	Netherlands

```
table {
filter:progid:DXImageTransform.Microsoft.Gradient(startColorstr='#DFE7F2',
endColorstr='#FFFFFF', gradientType='0');
}
```

For more information about filters, see "How do I use Internet Explorer's filters?" on page 32.

How do I use rounded table corners?

For Mozilla-based browsers (like Firefox), you can use the **-moz-border-radius** property to create a rounded table border.

Winner	Score	Loser
West Germany	1-0	Poland
Netherlands	2-0	Brazil
Poland	1-0	Brazil
West Germany	2-1	Netherlands

```
table {
  border: 1px solid #0000ff;
  -moz-border-radius: 8px;
  padding: 10px;
}
```

⚠ *The Mozilla-specific -moz-border-radius property is not supported by Internet Explorer, Opera, or Safari.*

How do I create boxes with rounded corners?

You can also use the **-moz-border-radius** property to add a curved border to any element, such as a paragraph.

Tip
See the "Positioning" chapter for tips about positioning a text box.

CSS rule
```
.curveBox {
  border: 1px solid #0000ff;
  -moz-border-radius: 25px;
  padding: 10px;
}
```

Usage
```
<div class="curveBox">your content</div>
```

The -moz-border-radius property only works in Mozilla-based browsers. For a cross-browser approach, you can use Alessandro Fulciniti's "Nifty Corners" approach:

CSS rules
```
.rounded { background: #c0c0c0; }

.rounded p {
  margin-left: 10px;
}

b.rTop, b.rBottom {
  display:block;
  background: #ffffff;
}

b.rTop b, b.rBottom b {
  display:block;
  height: 1px;
  overflow: hidden;
  background: #c0c0c0;
}
```

```
b.r1 { margin: 0 5px }
b.r2 { margin: 0 3px }
b.r3 { margin: 0 2px }

b.rTop b.r4, b.rBottom b.r4 {
  margin: 0 1px;
  height: 2px;
}
```

Usage
```
<div class="rounded">
 <b class="rTop">
  <b class="r1"></b><b class="r2"></b>
  <b class="r3"></b><b class="r4"></b>
 </b>
 <p>Tip ...</p>
 <b class="rBottom">
  <b class="r4"></b><b class="r3"></b>
  <b class="r2"></b><b class="r1"></b>
 </b>
</div>
```

Forms

You can create forms using the form tag. Within the form tag, you can add buttons, text boxes, larger text boxes called "text areas," checkboxes, and radio buttons.

How do I format buttons?

You can create buttons using the input or button tag. The following examples demonstrate how to change a button's background color and border and the button label's font family, font size, and font color.

> Send

CSS rule
```
input {
  font-family: Arial;
  font-size:12px;
  color: #ffffff;
  background-color: #0000ff;
  border-color: #ffff00;
}
```

Usage
```
<input type="submit" value="Send" />
```

CSS rule
```
button {
  font-family: Arial;
  font-size:12px;
  color: #ffffff;
  background-color: #0000ff;
  border-color: #ffff00;
}
```

Usage
```
<button>Send</button>
```

How do I add a background image to a button?

You can use the **background** property to add a background image to a button.

```
button { background:url('backImage.png'); }
```

You can position a background image on a button to include a label and an image on the button.

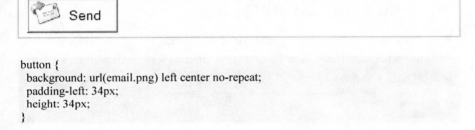

```
button {
    background: url(email.png) left center no-repeat;
    padding-left: 34px;
    height: 34px;
}
```

In this example, the image is 30px by 30px, so 34px of left padding is included to prevent the label from overlapping the image. The button has also been sized to 34px so the image will fit inside the button.

How do I format text areas and text boxes?

You can create text boxes using the input tag and text areas using the textarea tag. The following examples demonstrate how to change a text area and text box's background color, border, font family, font size, and text color.

To format a text box:

CSS rule

```
input {
  font-family: Arial;
  font-size:12px;
  color: #ffffff;
  background-color: #ff0000;
  border-color: #00ff00;
}
```

Usage

```
<input type="text" />
```

To format a text area:

CSS rule

```
textarea {
  font-family: Arial;
  font-size:12px;
  color: #ffffff;
  background-color: #ff0000;
  border-color: #00ff00;
}
```

Usage

```
<textarea rows="2" cols="40"></textarea>
```

How do I change a text box's background color when it's selected?

You can use the :focus pseudo class to change a text box or text area's background color when the user clicks inside the text box.

```
input:focus {
  background-color: #ffffc0;
  color: #000000;
}
```

How do I add a background image to a text area or text box?

You can add a background image to a text area or text box using the **background-image** property.

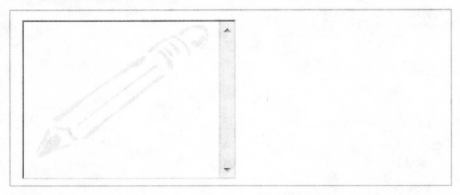

To add a background image to a text box:

input { background:url('pencil.gif') no-repeat; }

To add a background image to a text area:

CSS rule
textarea { background:url('pencil.gif') no-repeat; }

Usage
<textarea rows="24" cols="10"></textarea>

How do I format the scrollbar in a text area?

You can use the **scrollbar-arrow-color**, **scrollbar-base-color**, and **scrollbar-darkshadow-color** properties to format a text area's scrollbar.

```
textarea {
  scrollbar-arrow-color: #00ff00;
  scrollbar-base-color: #0000ff;
  scrollbar-darkshadow-color: #ff0000;
}
```

The scrollbar-darkshadow-color property is very subtle—it's applied to the border around the scrollbar arrows and the scroll box.

How do I format the scrollbar for the page?

You can also use the **scrollbar-arrow-color**, **scrollbar-base-color**, and **scrollbar-darkshadow-color** properties to format a page's scrollbar.

```
body {
  scrollbar-arrow-color: #00ff00;
  scrollbar-base-color: #0000ff;
  scrollbar-darkshadow-color: #ff0000;
}
```

How do I format checkboxes?

You can format a checkbox's background color and border.

☐ checkbox label

CSS rule
```
.cBox {
  background-color: #0000ff;
  border: 1px solid #ffff00;
}
```

Usage
```
<input type="checkbox" class="cBox" id="cBox1" />
<label for="cBox1">Checkbox 1</label>
```

How do I format radio buttons?

You can format a radio button's background color and border.

 radio button label

CSS rule
```
.rButton {
  background-color: #0000ff;
  border: 1px solid #ffff00;
}
```

Usage
```
<input type="radio" class="rButton" id="rbutton1" />
<label for="rbutton1">Radio button 1</label>
```

Print

You can create print-specific styles to format your content when users print a document.

How do I create a print style sheet?

You can create a separate style sheet for printing, or you can add a print section to your default style sheet.

You can use the **media** attribute to specify a print-specific style sheet for a page:

```
<link rel="stylesheet" type"text/css"
href="printstylesheetname.css" media="print">
```

Or, you can use the **@media** rule to include print-specific styles in a style sheet:

```
@media print { }
```

How do I prevent users from printing my page?

You can specify a blank document as the print style sheet.

```
<link rel="stylesheet" type"text/css"
href="blank.htm" media="print">
```

Your document (in this example, "blank.htm") could be completely blank, or it could tell users that they cannot print the page.

```
<?xml version="1.0" encoding="utf-8"?>
<html><head></head>
<body>
  <p>This page cannot be printed.</p>
</body>
</html>
```

Users could save the page and remove your print style sheet reference, but most users won't go to that much trouble.

How do I set the page margins for print?

You can use the margin properties to set the page margins in print.

```
@media print {
 body {
   margin-top: 1in;
   margin-right: .25in;
   margin-bottom: 1in;
   margin-left: .25in;
 }
}
```

You can use CSS shorthand to write this declaration as:

```
body { margin: 1in .25in 1in .25in}
```

The order is top right bottom left (clockwise).

If the margins are the same, you can simply use:

```
body { margin: .25in }
```

How do I change the font color to black for print?

You can use the universal selector and the **!important** keyword to set the color for all text.

```
@media print {
 * { color: black !important; }
}
```

How do I use a different font for print?

You can use the universal selector and the **!important** keyword to set the font family for all elements. This approach will work even if you have specified a font family for a specific tag, such as p (paragraphs).

```
@media print {
  * { font-family: times !important; }
}
```

How do I specify page breaks?

You can use the **page-break-before**, **page-break-after**, and **page-break-inside** properties to include or avoid page breaks.

To include page breaks before all heading 1s:

```
h1 { page-break-before: always; }
```

To avoid page breaks inside a table:

```
p { page-break-inside: avoid; }
```

⚠️ *The page-break-inside property is not supported when printing from Internet Explorer or Safari. It is supported by Firefox and Opera. None of these browsers correctly supports the page-break-inside property for tables.*

How do I repeat table headings across printed pages?

You can set the thead tag's **display** property to "table-header-group" to make a table header repeat when a table wraps across printed pages.

```
@media print {
  thead { display: table-header-group; }
}
```

How do I keep paragraphs on the same page?

You can use the **orphans** and **widows** properties to keep the lines of a paragraph on the same printed page.

An orphan is text that appears at the bottom of a page while the rest of the content continues on the next page.

text text text text text text text text text text text text text text text
text text text text text text text text text text text text text text text
text text text text text text text text text text text text text text text

This is an orphan. The rest of this paragraph is on the next page.

```
p { orphans: 3; }
```

A widow is text that appears on the next page while the rest of the content appeared on the previous page.

This is a widow. The rest of this paragraph is on the previous page.

```
p { widows: 3; }
```

Orphans and widows are set to "2" by default.

⚠ *Internet Explorer, Firefox, and Safari do not support the orphan and widow properties. However, they are both supported by Opera.*

How do I include link locations in print?

You can use the **content** property to include a link's location in print.

Click here to visit our website (http://www.clickstart.net/).

```
@media print {
  a:after { content: " (" attr(href) ")" }
}
```

How do I hide content when the user prints the page?

You can use the **display** property to hide content that you don't want to appear when the user prints the page.

CSS rule
```
@media print {
  .onlineOnly { display: none; }
}
```

Usage
```
<p class="onlineOnly">This paragraph will not print.</p>
```

Page layout

You can use CSS to set margins, create columns, add headers and footers, and overlap content.

What is the difference between margins and padding?

The **margin** properties add space to the *outside* of an element.

The **padding** properties add space *inside* the element—between its borders and its content.

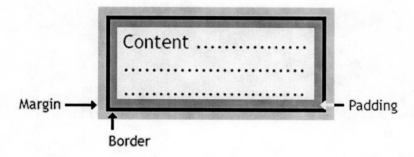

How do I center a block of content?

You can use the **text-align** property to center a block of content.

CSS rule
p.blockQuote { text-align: center; }

Usage
<p class="blockQuote">text</p>

How do I specify a block of content's position?

You can use the **position** property to specify a block of content's location.

If the position property is set to "absolute," the element's position has no effect on the positioning of other elements on the page. For example, two absolutely positioned elements can be positioned on top of each other:

> box 2̸

CSS rule
```
.box {
  position: absolute;
  top: 100px;
  left: 100px;
}
```

Usage
```
<div class="box"><p>box 1</p></div>
<div class="box"><p>box 2</p></div>
```

If the position is set to "relative," the second box appears below the first box:

> box 1
> box 2

CSS rule
```
.box {
  position: relative;
  top: 100px;
  left: 100px;
}
```

Usage
```
<div class="box"><p>box 1</p></div>
<div class="box"><p>box 2</p></div>
```

Since the "box 2" div is under the "box 1" div in the code, it must display under box 1.

How do I position content based on another block's position?

Blocks of content are positioned based on their container. If you place a div inside another div, its position will be based on the position of the container div.

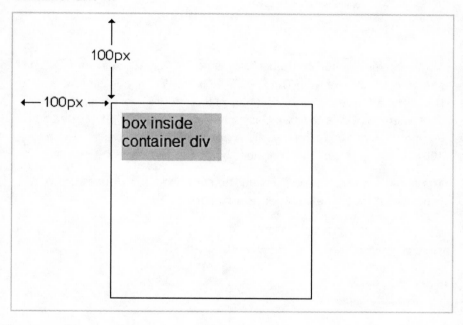

CSS rules
```
.container {
  position: absolute;
  top: 100px;
  left: 100px;
  width: 200px;
  height: 200px;
  border: 1px #000000 solid;
}
```

```
.box {
  position: relative;
  top: 10px;
  left: 10px;
  width: 100px;
  height: 50px;
  background: #aabbff;
}
```

Usage
```
<div class="container">
  <div class="box">
    <p>box inside container div</p>
  </div>
</div>
```

In this example, the "container" div is positioned 100px from the top and 100px from the left. The "box" div is inside the container div, so it is positioned based on the top (100px) left (100px) corner of the container div. Since the box class specifies a top position of 10px and a left position of 10px, the box div is positioned 10px from the top and 10px from the left of the container box's top left corner.

The box div is not "locked" inside the container, it just uses the container div's top left corner as a starting point:

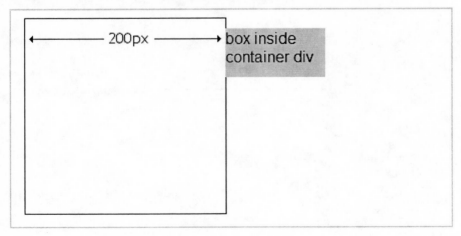

```
.container {
  position: absolute;
  top: 100px;
  left: 100px;
  width: 200px; height: 200px;
  border: 1px #000000 solid;
}

.box {
  position: relative;
  top: 10px;
  left: 200px;
  width: 100px; height: 50px;
  background: #aabbff;
}
```

Usage

```
<div class="container">
  <div class="box">
    <p>box inside container div</p>
  </div>
</div>
```

As you can see in the screenshot, the "box inside container div" is no longer inside the container. However, it is still positioned 200px from the left edge of the container, not the left edge of the page.

This approach makes moving a container div and its contents very easy. If you change the container's top, left, bottom, or right properties, all of the content inside of it will move too.

How do I position an image beside a paragraph?

You can use the **float** property to position an image to the left or right of a paragraph.

 sample text sample text sample text sample text sample text sample text sample text sample text sample text sample text sample text sample text sample text sample text sample text sample text sample text

CSS rules

```
.caution {
  float: left;
  padding-right: 10px;
}
```

Usage

```
<p><img src="../caution.png" class="caution" />
sample text ... sample text</p>
```

How do I float text on an image?

You can use the **top, right, bottom,** and **left** properties with the **position** property to float text on an image.

In this example, the text is moved up using a negative top value ("-200px").

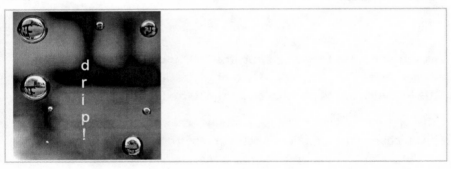

CSS rules

```
.overlap {
  position: relative;
  top: -200px;
  left: 180px;
  margin-left: 10px;
  color: #ffffff;
  font-size:24pt;
}
```

Usage

```
<img src="../images/drip.jpg" />
<p class="overlap">d<br />r<br />i<br />p<br />!</p>
```

How do I create a two-column layout: fixed left and fixed right?

You can create a fixed two-column layout by placing your content in two divs and setting each div's width using a fixed measurement unit, such as pixels. By setting the **float** property to "left," the two columns will be positioned beside each other.

You also need to set the body tag's width to the combined width of your two columns. In this example, the left column is set to 200px, the right column is set to 400px, and the body is set to 600px.

CSS rules
```
body { width: 600px; }

#leftSide {
  float: left;
  width: 200px;
  height: 100%;
  background: #f4f4f4;
}
#rightSide {
  float: left;
  width: 400px;
  height: 100%;
  background: #ddeeff;
}
```

Usage
```
<div id="leftSide"><p>left ... left</p></div>
<div id="rightSide"><p>right ... right</p></div>
```

How do I create a two-column layout: fixed left and fluid right?

A fluid column will resize based on the size of the browser window. If you specify a fixed width for the first column and don't specify a width for the second column, the second column will be fluid and resize.

In this example, we are creating a fixed left column and a fluid right column. The left column is set to a width of 200px, so it will not resize when the window is resized. The right column's width is not set, so it will automatically expand or collapse as the window is resized.

⚠ *In this layout, the right column will "disappear" if the browser window is sized to the width of the left column.*

| left left left left left left left left | right right right right right right right right

<- expands as the window is resized -> |

CSS rules
```
#leftSide {
  float: left;
  width: 200px;
  height: 100%;
  padding: 20px;
  background-color: #f4f4f4;
}
#rightSide {
  height: 100%;
  padding: 20px;
  background-color: #aabbff;
}
```

Usage
```
<div id="leftSide"><p>left ... left</p></div>
<div id="rightSide"><p>right ... right</p></div>
```

How do I create a two-column layout: fluid left and fixed right?

Creating a fluid (expandable) left column and a fixed right column is slightly more complex than creating a fixed left column and expanding right column. If you wrap the left column with another div, you can use the **margin-right** and **margin-left** properties to position the columns.

left left left left left left left left	right right right right right right right right
<- expands as the window is resized ->	

CSS rules

```
#leftWrapper {
  float: left;
  width: 100%;
  background: #ff00ff;
}

#leftSide {
  margin-right: 200px;
  /* set right margin to right column's width */
}

#rightSide {
  float: left;
  width: 200px;
  margin-left: -200px;
  background: #00ff00;
  /* set left margin to this column's width */
}
```

Usage

```
<div id="leftWrapper">
  <div id="leftSide"><p>left left ... left</p></div>
</div>
<div id="rightSide"><p>right ... right</p></div>
```

How do I create a two-column layout: fluid left and fluid right?

You can create a completely fluid two-column layout by specifying both columns' widths using percentages. Since percentage widths are based on the width of the window, they automatically resize as the window is resized.

CSS rules
```
#leftSide {
  float: left;
  width:20%; height: 100%;
  padding: 10px;
  background-color: #f4f4f4;
}

#rightSide {
  padding: 10px;
  width:80%; height: 100%;
  background-color: #aabbff;
}
```

Usage
```
<div id="leftSide"><p>left ... left</p></div>
<div id="rightSide"><p>right ... right</p></div>
```

How do I center a two-column layout?

You can center a two-column layout by wrapping the columns with a div that is centered.

To center the wrapper div, set its **left** property to "25%" and its **width** property to "50%."

To align the columns inside the div, set the left column's left property to 0% and the right column's right property to 0%. Each column's position property should be set to "absolute" so that it does not influence the other column's position.

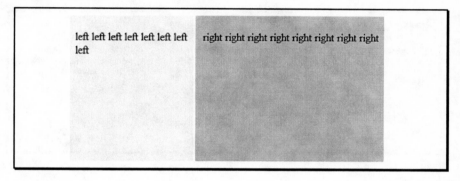

CSS rules

```
#wrapper {
  position: relative;
  height: 100%;
  left: 25%;
  width: 50%;
}

#leftSide {
  position: absolute;
  left: 0%;
  width: 40%; height: 100%;
  background-color: #f4f4f4;
}

#rightSide {
  position: absolute;
  right: 0%;
  width: 60%; height: 100%;
  background-color: #aabbff;
}
```

```
<div id="wrapper">
<div id="leftSide"><p>left ... left</p></div>
<div id="rightSide"><p>right ... right</p></div>
</div>
```

How do I create a three-column layout?

You can create a three-column layout by placing your content inside three div tags and setting the **float** property to "left." To prevent your columns from wrapping, you will need to set the width of the body tag.

Page title

left left left left left left left   middle middle middle middle middle   right right right right right
left left left left left left   middle middle middle middle middle   right right right right right
                                                                              right right right right right

CSS rules
```
body { width: 800px; }

#leftSide {
  float: left;
  width: 200px;
  height: 100%;
  background: #f4f4f4;
}

#middle {
  float: left;
  width: 400px;
  height: 100%;
  background: #ffffff;
}

#rightSide {
  float: left;
  width: 200px;
  height: 100%;
  background: #f4f4f4;
}
```

```
<div id="leftSide"><p>left ... left</p></div>
<div id="middle"><p>middle ... middle</p></div>
<div id="rightSide"><p>right ... right</p></div>
```

How do I add a header or footer?

You can add a header or footer by adding content above or below the column div tags.

CSS rules
```
body { width: 700px; }

#leftSide {
  float: left;
  width: 200px; height: 100%;
  background: #f4f4f4;
}

#rightSide {
  float: left;
  width: 400px; height: 100%;
  background: #ddeeff;
}
```

Usage
```
<h1>header ... header</h1>
<div id="leftSide"><p>left ... left</p></div>
<div id="rightSide"><p>right ... right</p></div>
<p>foot ... foot</p>
```

If the body tag's width is not set or is set to a size larger than the columns' combined width, the footer will wrap to the right of the second column. You can place the footer in a div and use the float property to prevent it from wrapping.

CSS rules
```
body { width: 700px; }

#leftSide {
  float: left;
  width: 200px;
  height: 100%;
  background: #f4f4f4;
}

#rightSide {
  float: left;
  width: 400px;
  height: 100%;
  background: #ddeeff;
}

#foot { float: clear; }
```

Usage
```
<h1>header ... header</h1>
<div id="leftSide"><p>left ... left</p></div>
<div id="rightSide"><p>right ... right</p></div>
<div id="foot"><p>foot ... foot</p></div>
```

How do I create a non-scrolling header?

You can create a non-scrolling header using the **position** and **overflow** properties.

In this example, the header has a height of 100px. If the browser window is very narrow, the header's content may not fit inside the header. Setting the overflow property to "hidden" hides the header content that doesn't fit within the header area.

header header header header header header header header header header header header
header header header header header header header header header header header header

text text text text text text text text text text text text text text text text text text text

text text text text text text text text text text text text text text text text text text text

text text text text text text text text text text text text text text text text text text text

text text text text text text text text text text text text text text text text text text text

text text text text text text text text text text text text text text text text text text text

CSS rules
```
body {
  margin: 0px;
  padding: 100px 0px 0px 0px;
  overflow: hidden;
/* overflow: hidden prevents full scrollbar in IE */
}

div#header {
/* you must include "div" for IE */
  position: absolute;
  top:0px;
  left: 0px;
  width: 100%;
  height: 100px;
  background-color: #aabbff;
  overflow: hidden;
}

#content {
  height: 100%;
  overflow: auto;
}
```

```
<div id="header"><p>header...header</p></div>
<div id="content"><p>text...text</p></div>
```

How do I create a non-scrolling footer?

You can create a non-scrolling footer using the **position** and **overflow** properties.

In this example, the footer has a height of 100px. If the browser window is very narrow, the footer's content may not fit inside the footer. The footer's overflow property is set to "hidden" to hide the content that doesn't fit.

text text text text text text text text text text text text text text text text text text text

text text text text text text text text text text text text text text text text text text text

text text text text text text text text text text text text text text text text text text text

text text text text text text text text text text text text text text text text text text text

text text text text text text text text text text text text text text text text text text text

footer footer footer footer

CSS rules
```
body {
  margin:0px;
  padding:0px 0px 100px 0px;
}

* html body { overflow: hidden; }
/* required for scrolling in IE */

#content {
  height: 100%;
  overflow: auto;
}

#footer {
  position: absolute;
  bottom: 0px;
  left: 0px;
  width: 100%;
```

```
  height: 100px;
  background-color: #aabbff;
  overflow: hidden;
}
```

Usage

```
<div id="content"><p>text...text</p></div>
<div id="footer"><p>footer...footer</p></div>
```

Testing

You will need to test your styles, especially since CSS support varies considerably across browsers.

Which browsers should I support?

Internet Explorer is the most commonly-used browser, but Firefox, Safari, and Opera are also popular. If possible, you should test your styles in all of these browsers. You can download free versions at the following websites.

Browser	Download site
Internet Explorer	www.microsoft.com/downloads
Firefox	www.mozilla.com/firefox
Opera	www.opera.com
Safari	www.apple.com/safari

Do I need to test in different operating systems?

There are sometimes bugs or inconsistencies that only appear in a browser on a specific operating system. If you have access to multiple operating systems, you should test your pages on a Windows, Mac, and Linux-based PC.

If you don't have access to different operating systems, you can view your site in different browsers on different operating systems at www.browsercam.com.

Can I install multiple versions of Internet Explorer in Windows?

Internet Explorer 8 includes an option to emulate IE7. If you need to test in IE6, you can download Microsoft's "Internet Explorer Application Compatibility VPC Image" at www.microsoft.com.

What tools can I use to test styles?

The following recommended tools can be used to test styles.

Tool	How you can use it	Download site
Optool	Open a page in any browser , then right-click to it in another browser	www.kreacom.dk
DOM Inspector	Examine an object's cascade order and applied styles (Mozilla-based browsers only)	www.mozilla.org
Firebug	Examine your styles and make live changes	www.getfirebug.com
Web Accessibility Toolbar	Validate your styles and make live changes	www.visionaustralia.org.au

How can I validate my style sheet?

You can use the W3C's CSS validation service at:

jigsaw.w3c.org/css-validator

The W3C's validator will check your style sheet for errors and make sure that it complies with the CSS recommendation.

What are some common CSS mistakes?

Five common style mistakes include:

1 Incorrect syntax

Your rules must use the following format:

```
selector { property: value; }
```

The properties can be written on multiple lines, but they should end with a semicolon and be contained within curly braces.

2 Invalid class and ID names

Class and ID names must begin with a letter, not a number or an underscore. They are also case sensitive.

3 Font name capitalization and spaces

Font names are case sensitive. If you specify a font with a multiple-word name, such as "Trebuchet MS," you must include quotes around its name.

```
p { font-family: "Trebuchet MS"; }
```

4 Typos

Make sure your property, tag, and class names don't include typos. Validating your style sheet will help you find typos.

5 Missing # from color hex values

Colors are usually specified using hex values, such as #ffffff. The hex value must include the # sign.

What are Acid1 and Acid2?

Acid1 and Acid2 were developed by the Web Standards Project, a group of web developers who encourage browser companies to create standards-compliant browsers. Acid1 and Acid2 are tests to determine how well a browser supports CSS.

To see how different browsers performed on each test, see:

en.wikipedia.org/wiki/Acid1

en.wikipedia.org/wiki/Acid2

Which CSS properties are supported by Internet Explorer?

The following website provides a list of CSS properties that are supported in Internet Explorer:

msdn2.microsoft.com/en-us/library/cc351024(VS.85).aspx

Which CSS properties are supported by Firefox?

The following website provides a list of CSS properties that are supported in Firefox:

developer.mozilla.org/en/docs/CSS_Reference

Which CSS properties are supported by Opera?

The following website provides a list of CSS properties that are supported in Opera:

www.opera.com/docs/specs/css/

Which CSS properties are supported by Safari?

The following website provides a list of CSS properties that are supported in Safari:

developer.apple.com/internet/safari/safari_css.html

How do I research browser-based CSS bugs?

If you think you've found a CSS bug, you should first verify your style sheet to make sure it's written correctly. You can validate your style sheet at:

jigsaw.w3c.org/css-validator

If your style sheet is valid, open your page in another browser to see if it displays as expected.

If your style sheet displays correctly in another browser, check the CSS-discuss wiki's browser bugs page to see if there's a problem with your browser:

css-discuss.incutio.com/?page=BrowserBugs

How do I specify style properties specifically for Internet Explorer?

You can use the underscore CSS hack to specify style properties for Internet Explorer only.

In this example, paragraphs will be red in Internet Explorer and green in all other browsers.

```
p {
  color: green;
  _color: red;
}
```

This approach is recognized by the W3C, so it will validate with the CSS validator. For more information, see :

www.w3.org/TR/CSS21/syndata.html#tokenization

There are many CSS hacks and filters that take advantage of bugs in various browsers. If possible, you should avoid using these hacks and filters. They could easily cause problems with future versions when the bugs are fixed. If you really need to specify a style property for a specific browser, see:

css-discuss.incutio.com/?page=CssHack

How do I override inline and embedded styles?

You can include the !important keyword in a style rule to override inline and embedded styles.

For example, the following declaration in a style sheet will make paragraphs black, even if an embedded or inline style specifies a different color.

```
p { color: black !important; }
```

The line above would override this embedded formatting:

```
<style>
 p { color: red; }
</style>
```

and this inline formatting:

```
<p style="color: yellow">text text text</p>
```

If you need to override multiple properties, you will need to include !important for each property.

```
p {
  font-family: Arial !important;
  color: red !important;
}
```

Resources

Want to learn more about CSS? There are some excellent online resources and books available.

Are there any free tools I can use to create style sheets?

The following free tools are very useful when designing styles and creating style sheets.

Tool	How you can use it	Download site
JR Screen Ruler	Measure distances onscreen to determine margins, widths, and heights	www.spadixbd.com
TopStyle Lite	Develop style sheets and view style properties	www.bradsoft.com
Layout-o-Matic	Select your desired options and automatically create a multi-column site layout	www.inknoise.com

Where can I view the CSS standard?

Cascading style sheets are a recommendation of the World Wide Web Consortium (W3C). You can view and download the recommendation at:

www.w3.org/Style/CSS

Which books do you recommend?

I recommend the following CSS books:

Cascading Style Sheets: Designing for the Web
Hakon Lie and Bert Bos

CSS Anthology: 101 Essential Tips, Tricks & Hacks
Rachel Andrew

CSS Mastery: Advanced Web Standards Solutions
Andy Budd, Simon Collison, and Cameron Moll

CSS Web Site Design Hands on Training
Eric Meyer

Which CSS websites do you recommend?

The **CSS-Discuss** wiki (css-discuss.incutio.com) is an excellent archive of CSS bugs, techniques, tutorials, and demonstrations.

Also, the **css-discuss** mailing list (www.css-discuss.org) is a great way to discuss CSS and ask questions.

Are there any cool CSS example sites on the Web?

The **CSS Zen Garden** (www.csszengarden.com) provides inspiring CSS examples. Designers download a sample page and use CSS to design the page. The variety and creativity are very impressive—highly recommended!

CSS Beauty (www.cssbeauty.com) has a collection of real-world examples of CSS.

CSS Quick Reference

Default values are listed first and appear in bold. A values of "n/a" indicates that the property does not have a default value.

✓ - supported

✗ - not supported

Background and Color properties

Name	Values	Inherited?	IE	Firefox	Opera	Safari
background	**see property defaults** any of the background properties	no	buggy	✓	✓	✓
background-attachment	**scroll** fixed	no	buggy	✓	✓	✓
background-color	**transparent** [color]	no	buggy	✓	✓	✓
background-image	**none** [uri]	no	buggy	✓	✓	✓
background-position	**0% 0%** [percentage] [length] center top right bottom left	no	✓	✓	✓	✓
background-repeat	**repeat** repeat-x repeat-y no-repeat	no	✓	✓	✓	✓
color	**browser-dependent** [color]	yes	✓	✓	✓	✓

Border and Outline properties

Name	Values	Inherited?	IE	Firefox	Opera	Safari
border	**n/a** border-width border-style border-color	no	buggy	✓	✓	✓
border-collapse	**collapse** separate	yes	✓	✓	✓	✓
border-color	**color property value** [color] transparent	no	buggy	✓	✓	✓
border-spacing	**0** [length]	yes	✗	✓	✓	✓
border-style	see individual style properties	no	buggy	✓	✓	✓
border-top border-right border-bottom border-left	**n/a** border-top-width border-style [color]	no	buggy	✓	✓	✓
border-top-color border-right-color border-bottom-color border-left-color	**color property value** [color] transparent inherit	no	buggy	✓	✓	✓
border-top-style border-right-style border-bottom-style border-left-style	**none** dotted dashed solid double	no	buggy	✓	✓	✓

Name	Values	Inherited?	IE	Firefox	Opera	Safari
	groove ridge inset outset hidden inherit					
border-top-width border-right-width border-bottom-width border-left-width	**medium** thin thick inherit [length]	no	buggy	✓	✓	✓
border-width	**medium** thin thick inherit [length]	no	buggy	✓	✓	✓
outline	**none** any of the outline properties	no	✗	✓	✓	✓
outline-color	**invert** [color] inherit	no	✗	✓	✓	✓
outline-style	**none** same as the border values	no	✗	✓	✓	✓
outline-width	**medium** thin thick inherit [length]	no	✗	✓	✓	✓

Generated Content properties

Name	Values	Inherited?	IE	Firefox	Opera	Safari
counter	**normal** inhert [uri] [string] open-quote close-quote no-open-quote no-close-quote attr([attribute name]) counter([name], [style])	no	✕	partial	partial	partial
counter-increment	**none** inherit [counter name][number]	no	✕	✓	buggy	✕
counter-reset	**none** inherit [counter name][number]	no	✕	✓	✓	✕
quotes	**browser-dependent** <string> none	yes	✕	✓	buggy	✕

List properties

Name	Values	Inherited?	IE	Firefox	Opera	Safari
list-style	**individual property defaults** list-style-type list-style-position list-style-image	yes	buggy	✓	✓	✓
list-style-image	**none** [uri]	yes	buggy	✓	✓	✓
list-style-position	**outside** inside	yes	✓	✓	✓	✓
list-style-type	**disc** circle square decimal decimal-leading-zero lower-roman upper-roman lower-greek lower-alpha lower-latin upper-alpha upper-latin hebrew armenian georgian cjk-ideographic hiragana katakana hiragana-iroha katakana-iroha none	yes	buggy	✓	✓	✓

Margin and Padding properties

Name	Values	Inherited?	IE	Firefox	Opera	Safari
margin	0 [length] [percentage] auto inherit	no	buggy	✓	✓	✓
margin-top margin-right margin-bottom margin-left	0 [length] [percentage] auto inherit	no	buggy	✓	✓	✓
padding	0 [length] [percentage] inherit	no	✓	✓	✓	✓
padding-top padding-right padding-bottom padding-left	0 [length] [percentage] inherit	no	✓	✓	✓	✓

Page Layout properties

Name	Values	Inherited?	IE	Firefox	Opera	Safari
bottom	**auto** [length] [percentage]	no	✓	✓	✓	✓
clear	**none** left right both	no	buggy	✓	✓	✓
clip	**auto** rect([top] [right][bottom] [left]) inherit	no	partial	✓	✓	✓
float	**none** left right	no	buggy	buggy	buggy	✓
left	**auto** [length] [percentage]	no	✓	✓	✓	✓
overflow	**visible** hidden scroll auto	no	✓	✓	✓	✓
position	**static** relative absolute fixed	no	buggy	✓	✓	✓
right	**auto** [length] [percentage]	no	✓	✓	✓	✓

Name	Values	Inherited?	IE	Firefox	Opera	Safari
top	**auto** [length] [percentage]	no	✓	✓	✓	✓
visibility	**inherit** visible hidden collapse	no	partial	✓	partial	buggy
z-index	**auto** [integer]	no	buggy	buggy	✓	✓

Print properties

Name	Values	Inherited?	IE	Firefox	Opera	Safari
orphans	**2** any positive integer	yes	✕	✕	✓	✕
page-break-after	**auto** always avoid left right	no	partial	partial	✓	partial
page-break-before	**auto** always avoid left right	no	partial	partial	✓	partial
page-break-inside	**auto** avoid	yes	✕	✕	✓	✕
widows	**2** any positive integer	yes	✕	✕	✓	✕

Size properties

Name	Values	Inherited?	IE	Firefox	Opera	Safari
height	**auto** [length] [percentage]	no	✓	✓	✓	✓
max-height	**none** [length] [percentage]	no	✓	✓	✓	✓
max-width	**none** [length] [percentage]	no	✓	✓	✓	✓
min-height	default: 0 [length] [percentage]	no	✓	✓	✓	✓
min-width	default: varies [length] [percentage]	no	✓	✓	✓	✓
width	**auto** [length] [percentage]	no	✓	✓	✓	✓

Table properties

Name	Values	Inherited?	IE	Firefox	Opera	Safari
border-collapse	**collapse** separate	yes	✓	✓	✓	✓
border-spacing	**0** [length]	yes	✗	✓	✓	✓
caption-side	**top** bottom left right	yes	✓	✓	✓	✓
empty-cells	**show** hide	yes	✗	buggy	buggy	✓
table-layout	**auto** fixed	no	✓	✓	✓	✓

Typographical properties

Name	Values	Inherited?	IE	Firefox	Opera	Safari
direction	**ltr** **(left to right)** rtl (right to left)	yes	✓	✓	✓	✓
font	**see individual** **properties** font-style font-variant font-weight font-size/line-height font-family	yes	✓	✓	✓	✓
font-family	**browser-** **dependent** [font family name] [multiple font names]	yes	✓	✓	✓	✓
font-size	**medium** inherit [percentage] [length] larger smaller xx-small x-small small large x-large xx-large	yes	✓	✓	✓	✓
font-style	**normal** italic oblique	yes	✓	✓	✓	✓

Name	Values	Inherited?	IE	Firefox	Opera	Safari
font-variant	**normal** small-caps	yes	✓	✓	✓	✗
font-weight	**normal** bold bolder lighter 100, 200,...900	yes	✓	✓	✓	✓
letter-spacing	**normal** [length]	yes	✓	✓	✓	✓
line-height	**normal** [number] [length] [percentage]	yes	buggy	✓	✓	✓
text-align	**browser-dependent** left right center justify <string>	yes	buggy	✓	✓	✓
text-decoration	**none** underline overline line-through blink	no	buggy	buggy	✓	✓
text-indent	default: 0 [length] [percentage]	yes	✓	✓	✓	✓
text-transform	**none** capitalize uppercase lowercase	yes	buggy	✓	✓	✓

Name	Values	Inherited?	IE	Firefox	Opera	Safari
vertical-align	**baseline** sub super top text-top middle bottom text-bottom [percentage] [length]	no	buggy	buggy	✓	✓
white-space	**normal** pre nowrap	yes	partial	partial	partial	✓
unicode-bidi	**normal** embed bidi-override	no	buggy	✓	✓	✗
word-spacing	**normal** [length]	yes	✓	buggy	buggy	✓

Index

!important keyword, 18, 100, 101, 128
* (universal selector), 14
:active pseudo class, 61, 62, 63
:after pseudo element, 46, 47, 60, 103
:before pseudo element, 46, 47, 57, 58, 59, 60
:focus pseudo class, 61, 66, 95
:hover pseudo class, 61, 62, 63, 87
:link pseudo class, 62
:visited pseudo class, 62, 63
@media print rule, 64, 99, 100, 101, 103
<link> element, 13
Acid1 CSS browser test, 126
Acid2 CSS browser test, 126
Auto-numbering, 59
Background images
  adding, 71
  multiple, 74
  nonscrolling, 73
  positioning, 71
background property, 28, 67, 88, 94
background-attachment property, 73
background-color property, 23, 63
background-image property, 71, 96
background-position property, 71, 72
Books
  recommended, 130
border property, 57, 67, 76
border-bottom property, 29, 63
border-collapse property, 82
Borders
  adding a list, 57
  adding to images, 76
  formatting table borders, 81, 82
border-style property, 81, 82, 83
Bos, Bert, 11
bottom property, 109, 110
Boxes
  with rounded corners, 90

Browsers
  Acid tests, 126
  Firefox CSS support, 126
  Internet Explorer CSS support, 126
  Internet Explorer-specific styles, 127
  Opera CSS support, 126
  Safari CSS support, 127
  supporting, 123
  testing, 123
Bulleted lists, 49
  adding borders, 57
  adjusting the space between the bullet and the content, 57
  changing the bullet icon, 53
  formatting nested lists, 49
  formatting one item differently, 51
  formatting the first item differently, 52
  left-aligning, 54
  setting margins for a list, 50
  setting margins for list items, 51
Buttons
  formatting, 93, 94
Capitalizing text, 28
Centering, 105
Centering text, 26
Checkboxes
  formatting, 97
Classes, 15
color property, 23
Colors, 17
Comments, 19
Content
  inserting, 46
content property, 46, 47, 55, 57, 64, 103
counter property, 58, 59
counter-increment property, 59, 60
counter-reset property, 57, 59, 60
Cross out, 30

146 | Index

CSS training

ClickStart offers CSS training and consulting. You can also sign-up for our CSS Tips and Tricks email newsletter. For more information, visit our website at www.clickstart.net.

LaVergne, TN USA
31 March 2010

177728LV00004B/77/P